LEARNING WI

For six- to seven-year-olds

Go Away, Rose!

Story by Irene Yates
Activities by David Bell, Geoff Leyland,
Mick Seller and Irene Yates

Illustrations by Pauline Little

People who live in Cherry Walk

Mum Dad Steven Chris Harry Mum Dad Beverley

Baby Jenny Mark Kerry Charley Wesley Rose

Pusscuss

Boy

For MJ

It was such lovely weather. Everyone in Cherry Walk felt like going on holiday.

'Why don't we bring a holiday to Cherry Walk?' someone suggested.

Talk about what the children are doing in the picture.
What kind of mood do you think they are in?

What do you do on your summer holidays?
Do you ever get bored?

Play this game. Take it in turns to say 'We're going
away on holiday and taking a . . .' The other person
must remember what the first one has said and must add
an extra thing of their own. The winner is the person
who can remember the most things, in the right order.

No-one knew who thought of the holiday first. But Wesley had an even better idea.

'We could have a carnival!' he shouted.

'And we could raise lots of money for the hospital,' said Kerry.

4

How much do you think Wesley meant when he
talked about 'lots of money'?
Might it be £5, £50, £500 or even £5000?

Have you ever raised money for a good cause?
What did you do?
How much money did you make?

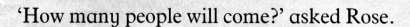

'How many people will come?' asked Rose.

'There's my mum and dad and your mum and dad . . .' began Kerry.

'Thousands, I expect,' said Charley. 'We'll need somewhere really big to fit them all in.'

'Cherry Manor!' cried Kerry, Wesley and Charley, all at once. 'Let's go and ask Ron.'

How many people are there in your class at school?

Do you know how many classes there are altogether?

Find out how many children there are in your school.

Are there thousands or hundreds?

They found Ron in the shrubbery.

Kerry thought it would be just the place for a treasure hunt.

'Cor!' said Charley.

Ron didn't fancy the idea at all.

How many birds' nests can you see in the picture?
What are they made of?

Do birds live in a nest all year round?
Where do some birds go in the winter?

In the spring try to watch a pair of nesting birds.
See what they carry in their beaks.
Count how often they visit the nest in a short
period of time.
Be careful not to disturb them.

If you have a book about birds, or can borrow one,
find out more about the birds you have seen.

9

Kerry said, 'We could have the music here.'

'My sister plays in an all-girl band!' said Wesley proudly.

'And we've got a band of our own,' added Charley.
'A rapping band. We can play really loud.'

'You can, can you,' said Ron.

Is it a sunny day in the picture?
Can you see any shadows?
Where are they?
Have you ever seen the shadow of a cloud?

Draw around a shadow, or place some
toys around its edge. Have a look at
the shadow every hour. What happens
to it? Never look directly at the sun.

Can you see something in the picture
which uses the sun and shadows to
tell the time?

Cherry Manor belonged to Miss Taylor.
'She won't like this at all,' muttered Ron.

But she did. 'A carnival's just the ticket!' she
cried, clapping her hands. 'We'll put up a tent.
And I'll make some cakes. And we'll have
scones and strawberry jam.'

Ask your mum or dad if you can help next time they make some cakes.
What goes into the cake? Help mix it up.
What does the mixture look like before it goes into the oven?
What colour is it? How does it feel?
How does it smell?

Have another look when the cake has been taken out of the oven and has cooled down.
What has happened to the mixture?
Has it changed colour?
Does it feel different?
Does it smell different?

Charley asked Dad what he thought about it.

'Great idea! You could have lots of stalls.
Tombola. Old books. White elephants.' Dad said.
'But you'll have to plan it properly.'

Rose's eyes sparkled. 'Can me and Mark look
after the elephants?'

14

You could play the game Rose and
Wesley are playing.
Collect six empty drinks cans.
Stack them into a pyramid.
Roll a ball at the cans.
How many can you knock down at once?

Try playing the game outside.
Here you can throw the ball.
Are you better at throwing with your
right or left hand?

Kerry decided to have a clear-out.

'I don't need these toys any longer,' she said. 'They can be treasure for the treasure hunt.'

Then she made a list of all the friends she had at school who might be able to give something.

Write down the names of your ten favourite toys.
Now write the list again but put the names in
alphabetical order – put any name beginning
with an 'a' first, then any beginning
with 'b', and so on.

Make up clues for a treasure hunt.
Play it in one room in your home.
You could start your first clue like this:

1 Clue 2 is under the t_____.

Hide the clue under something beginning
with 't', such as a table.

Put some real treasure at the end of your
treasure hunt!

17

Beverley was busy.
'I thought the girls in the band could wear
special costumes,' she said.
'Just like a real carnival!'

Kerry was *so* excited.
'Why don't we all dress up?
We could make lots of costumes and . . .'

'And me!' said Rose.
But nobody took any notice of her.

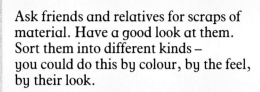

Ask friends and relatives for scraps of
material. Have a good look at them.
Sort them into different kinds –
you could do this by colour, by the feel,
by their look.

Look at your bits of material through a
magnifying glass. What can you see?

Make a collage picture with your material.

Beverley organised everyone in her band to sort out the old clothes and make the costumes. Rose tried to help.

'You're getting in the way, Rose!' Beverley said firmly.

You could decorate an old T-shirt with
cut-out shapes of material or paper.
What would make a clear pattern?
You could cut out lots of circles or
squares or triangles.
Use all sorts of different colours.
Stick your shapes on the T-shirt
with glue.

What about trying some different shapes?

You could try a pentagon

Or a hexagon

What should the band play?
Out came all their music. Out came their songs.
Out came their instruments.

Rose wanted to play too.

'Don't you dare!' Beverley warned her.

Look at the instruments in the picture.
How many can you name?
What sort of noise do you think they
will make?

Collect together pictures of instruments
from old magazines.
Try to put them into groups.

Charley and Wesley made up a new rap
and sang it to Kerry.

Kerry joined in.
Rose wanted to join in too.

'Go away, Rose!' Charley said.
'Yes, go away, Rose!' Wesley echoed.

See how quietly you can talk and
still be heard.
How loudly can you talk?

What happens to your voice when you talk
into a cardboard tube?

Make a cone shape from a piece of paper.
Cut off the point so that you can talk
into it.
What does this do to your voice?

'Hey! That's not a bad rap!' Beverley called, and she started to play a backing to it.

The new band got a huge round of applause.

How many different sounds can you make without an instrument?

Clap your hands together.
Clap using one, two and three fingers.

Clap using your nails.
Rub your nails together.
Try clicking your fingers together.

Tap your arms, legs or chest.
Do they make a different sound?

See if you can whistle.

27

Rose burst into tears and rushed into
her daddy's arms.

'Not fair!' she cried. 'Rose wants to dress up!
Rose wants to sing! Not fair!'

Desmond let out a laugh. 'Wait here a minute,'
he said. 'I've got just the thing for you!'

Why is Rose sulking? Why does Desmond laugh?
How do you think the rest of the children
feel about Rose?

Do you have a little brother or sister?
Do you get cross with them sometimes?

Look back in the story to see all the naughty
things Rose was doing. Draw a picture of one
of the things and show it to someone in
your family. Explain what it is about.

29

Rose couldn't believe her eyes.

'All the way from America!' Desmond smiled. 'And just the thing to make my little Rose queen of the Cherry Manor carnival.'

Rose smiled. Queen Rose! Nobody would ever be able to boss her about again!

See if you can copy the pattern on the costume
on to a piece of paper. Remember to use exactly
the same shapes and colours.

Draw a picture of a costume you would like to
wear to a carnival. Give it a lovely pattern.

Activity notes

Pages 2–3   Memory and language games help children to concentrate and to listen more closely. You can vary the game by using items beginning with a specific sound or letter.

Pages 4–5   Children often have a very hazy understanding of large amounts of money. £50 and £5,000 may both be seen as 'a lot of money'. You can help your child learn about the relative value of things by talking about prices when you are shopping together.

Pages 6–7   Encouraging your child to guess before finding out the actual numbers will develop useful estimating skills.

Pages 8–9   This activity involves close observation of birds nesting, and will help children to understand the diversity of birds and their nesting habits, eg shape and size, materials and location. Make sure your child understands that birds are easily upset if their nests are touched or watched too obviously.

Pages 10–11   This simple investigation involves noting changes in shadows during the course of a sunny day. At a later stage, children will learn that, as the earth spins, the sun *appears* to move through the sky. If you repeat the experiment on another sunny day, your child will begin to see that this movement is regular.

Pages 12–13   This activity is about noticing how things change when they are cooked. It encourages children to focus on different kinds of change by using the senses of smell, taste, touch and sight.

Pages 14–15   Children should soon realise that they can throw more accurately with one hand than the other. Think about what else you could use to knock down the cans. You could try making small fabric bags, about 10 cm square. Suggest your child fills them with dried rice, dried peas, marbles or feathers. Which bag is best for knocking down the cans? Ask your child to guess before beginning.

Pages 16–17   Alphabetical order is central to learning study skills at a later stage. Make learning the alphabet fun by playing different games such as treasure hunting, I-Spy, etc.

Pages 18–19   Here your child is looking closely at different kinds of material. Can they see the criss-cross patterns of the weave when they look through the magnifying glass? There are many good craft games available which will involve children in doing some weaving of their own if they are interested.

Pages 20–21   Playing around with two-dimensional shapes will help your child to learn about their properties, eg the number of sides, whether they have right angles, whether they tessellate (fit together exactly).

Pages 22–23   Talk together about the different ways in which the magazine pictures can be arranged into groups. They could be grouped according to size, colour, shape, or the way they are played. You could suggest your child makes a simple plucked instrument by stretching some elastic bands over a margarine container.

Pages 24–25   Encourage your child to predict what might happen before talking into the cardboard tube and the cone. Were they right? What happens when they use the cone to talk to a friend, but face the wrong way? You can also try to listen using the cone – what happens?

Pages 26–27   Your child might have some very imaginative ideas on how to make other sounds! Encourage them to describe the sounds – are they soft or loud, clear or fuzzy? What happens to some of the sounds if they put woollen gloves on?

Pages 28–29   Talking about how someone in a story feels and behaves can help children to identify and talk more easily about their own feelings. At a later stage this should help them make their own story-writing more true-to-life.

Pages 30–31   Looking closely at patterns is part of early maths. By doing this, your child will find it easier to see the similarities and differences between various numbers and shapes.

About the authors and advisers

Irene Yates is a writer and teacher in charge of language development at Lakey Lane School in Birmingham.

David Bell is Assistant Director of Education (Forward Planning) for Newcastle upon Tyne City Council, a former primary head and maths specialist.

Geoff Leyland is Deputy Head of Deer Park Primary School in Derbyshire and a former science and technology advisory teacher.

Mick Seller is Deputy Head of Asterdale Primary School in Derbyshire and a former science and technology advisory teacher.

Elizabeth Bassant is a language advisory teacher in Haringey, London. **Peter Ovens** is Principal Lecturer for Curriculum and Professional Development at Nottingham Polytechnic and a science specialist. **Peter Patilla** is a maths consultant, author and Senior Lecturer in Mathematics Education at Sheffield Polytechnic. **Margaret Williams** is an advisory teacher for maths in Newton Abbot, Devon.